POCKETBOOK OF FAITH 2

ANOTHER LITTLE BOOK OF ENCOURAGEMENT

ANTHONY SLUZAS

POCKETBOOK OF FAITH
Another Little Book of Encouragement

Anthony Sluzas

All rights reserved. No part of this book may be reproduced or transmitted in any form or by any means, electronic or mechanical, or information storage and retrieval system without written permission from the author.

Unless otherwise indicated, all Scripture quotations are taken from **New King James Version of the Holy Bible**, Copyright © 1982 by Thomas Nelson. Used by permission. All rights reserved.

All Scripture quotations marked KJV are taken from the **King James Version of the Holy Bible**, Public Domain.

All Scripture quotations marked NLT are taken from **The Holy Bible, New Living Translation** copyright © 1996, 2004, 2007 by the Tyndale House Foundation. Used by permission of Tyndale House Publishers, Inc., Carol Stream, Illinois 60188. All rights reserved.

All Scripture quotations marked TLB are taken from **The Living Bible** copyright © 1971 by Tyndale House Foundation. Used by permission of Tyndale House Publishers Inc., Carol Stream, Illinois 60188. All rights reserved.

All Scripture quotations from the New **American Standard Bible** are Copyright © 1960, 1962, 1963, 1968, 1971, 1972, 1973, 1975, 1977, 1995 by The Lockman Foundation. Used by permission.

All Scripture quotations from **The Message** are Copyright © 1993, 1994, 1995, 1996, 2000, 2001, 2002. Used by permission of NavPress Publishing Group.

All photos in this work are in the public domain and have been edited for this work.

Copyright © 2018 by Anthony Sluzas.

ISBN: 1725949008
13-Digit: 978-1725949003

Printed in the United States of America.

Cover and interior design by:
The Righteous Pen Publications Group
The righteousness of God shall guide my pen
www.righteouspenpublications.com

Dedicated to my grandsons, Carter & Nolan.
Always remember that Jesus loves you,
and so does Poppy.

– TABLE OF CONTENTS –

1	The Cross: The Alpha & Omega Of Faith....	1
2	Changes...	11
3	Worried Sick......................................	17
4	Eyeball To Eyeball With Fear.................	29
5	Speak!..	37
6	Hungry For More................................	43
7	Saying "Yes" To God's Plan...................	51
	References...	59
	About The Author...............................	61

But without faith *it is* impossible to please *Him,* for he who comes to God must believe that He is, and *that* He is a rewarder of those who diligently seek Him.
(Hebrews 11:6)

- CHAPTER 1 -

THE CROSS:
THE ALPHA & OMEGA OF FAITH

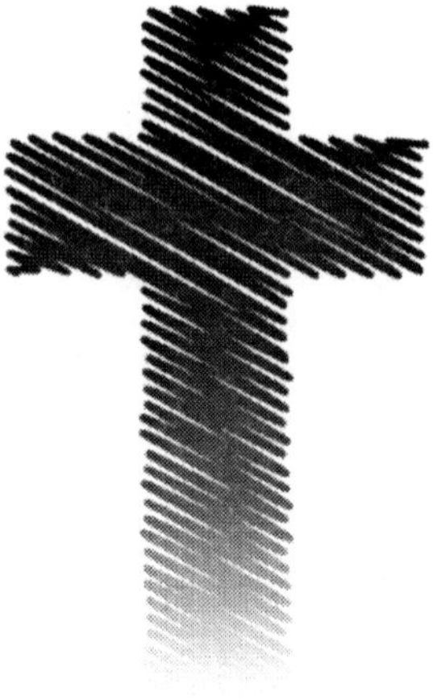

I am often asked how one can truly live a victorious life in these difficult days. The answer is found in your Bible.

We live in a day when the message of faith has been sabotaged, and driven off into a ditch of extremes. However, I am convinced that what the Lord is saying to His Church is, "Don't seek me so much for what I can do, but rather, seek Me for who I am."

This doesn't mean we shouldn't lay our needs before God, but instead, the emphasis must be placed on Who He is, rather than what He can do. It's not about some "cosmic Santa Claus" who is here to do our bidding. It's really all about intimacy; our relationship with our God.

In this intimate relationship with God, He wants us to always remember that:

- Everything that we believe, confess, and do must be in line with the Word of God, with no deviation.

- Remain plugged in to Christ, and He in you, no matter what.

He who says, I know Him, and keeps not His Commandments is a liar, and the Truth is not in him.
(1 John 2:4)

If your life is not changed by what is professed, then you really don't have what is professed.

But whosoever keeps His Word...in him verily is the love of God perfected; Hereby we know that we are in Him.

(1 John 2:5, KJV)

So how does one live for God; in victory and power? Here is the foundation of victory:

I have been crucified with Christ: it is no longer I who live, but Christ lives in me; and the life which I now live in the flesh I live by the Faith in the Son of God, who loved me and gave Himself for me. (Galatians 2:20)

If you have made Jesus Christ the Lord of your life, then you should know that you are saved by grace (unmerited favor), through faith. It is the *gift* of God, and not of works, lest anyone should boast (Ephesians 2:8, 9).

Grace, simply stated is the goodness of God, given to totally undeserving believers.

God's love, His amazing grace, and mercy were poured out on the earth as Jesus' life's blood was shed for us upon Calvary's cross.

His grace and saving power is still available to lost and dying humanity today. It is ours for the receiving...from the villager in the most remote part of the world, all the way to even the most bloodthirsty of dictators.

God has no more grace today than He did thousands of years ago. The truth is that He can now dispense grace in a much greater quantity than ever before, and all because of Calvary's cross.

And you, being dead in your trespasses...He has made alive together with Him, having forgiven you all trespasses, having wiped out the hand-writing of requirements that was against us, which was contrary to us. And He has taken it out of the way,

having it nailed to the cross.
(Colossians 2:14-15)

What Jesus accomplished on the Cross is the means by which grace is dispensed to all believers (Romans 6:3-5; 1 Corinthians 1:17-18, 23; 2:2).

In order for the grace of God to come to the believer in an uninterrupted flow, the believer must anchor his or her faith exclusively in Jesus Christ and His finished work for us on the Cross. If our faith is divided, then grace will be frustrated. And the end result will be a negative one indeed.

Rev. Jimmy Swaggart put together a brilliant outline which is such a blessing to meditate on, to preach, and to live by:

- **OUR FOCUS:** The Lord Jesus Christ (John 14:6)
- **THE OBJECT OF OUR FAITH:** The Cross of Christ & what He accomplished there (Romans 6:3-5).
- **OUR POWER SOURCE:** The Holy Spirit (Romans 8:1-2, 11).
- **THE RESULT:** Victory (Romans 6:14).[1]

Take a look at the same outline, but yet inverted by the belief system of much of modern "Churchianity."

- **OUR FOCUS:** Works (Ephesians 2:8-9).
- **THE OBJECT OF OUR FAITH:** Performance (Romans 7:9).
- **OUR POWER SOURCE:** Self (Luke 9:23).
- **THE RESULT:** Defeat (Galatians 5:4).[2]

If the believer doesn't understand the finished work of Jesus at Calvary's Cross, he is left with little more than his puny human willpower to thwart the attacks of Satan.

There is only one road to victory for the children of God, and that is by faith in Jesus Christ, and what He has done for us upon the Cross.

Again, see what Paul said regarding the importance of the Cross:

For Christ sent me not to baptize, but to preach the Gospel; not with wisdom of words, lest the Cross of Christ should be made of none effect.
(1 Corinthians 1:17, KJV)

Again, may I quote from Rev. Swaggart, "The Believer must place his faith exclusively in Christ and the Cross, understanding that Christ is always the Source of *all* things we receive from God, but that the Cross is the means by which these things are given to us. That's the reason we must have faith exclusively in Christ and the Cross. This being done, the Holy Spirit, Who superintends everything received from the Lord, will then have liberty to work within our hearts and lives, thereby bringing about the desired results, which He alone can do (Romans 8:2)."[3]

No, we do not have faith in our faith; our faith is completely focused upon Jesus (Hebrews 12:2).

There is no other means of victory over sin, sickness, demons, fear, and poverty, except by our faith placed exclusively in Christ and His finished work on the Cross.

It's about Jesus

What Jesus accomplished at the Cross is a finished work. Nothing can ever be added to it or taken away from it! This just irritates the fire out of religious folk because they are loath to give up their religion. What do we mean when we use the word, "religion?" Religion is any system invented by man in order to reach God, or to better oneself in some way. Man-concocted religion is something God can never accept. True Salvation originates with God. Man has nothing to do with it, with the exception of simply accepting what God has already done through Jesus Christ, His Son.

What does God's Word say?

As His divine power has given to us all things that pertain to life and godliness, through the knowledge of Him who called us by glory and virtue, by which have been given to us exceedingly great and precious promises, that through these you may be partakers of the divine nature, having escaped the corruption that is in the world through lust.
(2 Peter 1:3-4)

Either our Lord gave us everything, which He said He did, or else He didn't. You must choose to believe or disbelieve the Word of God given to you. But you must accept by faith that God said what He meant and meant what He said, in order to avail yourself of all the Word's privileges and blessings.

It is Jesus' finished work upon Calvary's Cross; alone, that stands between humankind and the Judgment of God. It is through Jesus' precious blood, and the power in His Name, that we receive authority over sin, sickness, demons, poverty, and fear. The Cross of Christ covers it all; spirit, soul, and body. This dominion and authority belongs to you if Jesus is the Lord of your life!

Sadly, in today's "enlightened" society, people are trying to discredit the Bible by removing the miraculous from its pages, and explaining away its moral precepts. If you hang out with such people or go to a church like this; Run! Get away from them! You can love, and pray for them...at a distance.

All things are possible; only believe

Please remember, dear one, that nothing is impossible with God. Any and all impossibility is with us when we measure God by the limitations of our unbelief.

One dear lady who I used to pastor always seemed to be so down in the dumps and terribly negative. She could see a dark cloud in every silver lining. One could greet her after a Sunday morning service with a "Isn't it a glorious morning?" and she would invariably respond with a litany of the latest woes and maladies that were plaguing her. Her mouth continually sabotaged what little faith she may have had. Life was a trial for her and her family; spiritually, financially, physically, mentally, and relationally. This dear sister's mouth was perpetuating the negativity in her life, and allowed the enemy quite a stronghold.

You are snared by the words of your mouth; you are taken by the words of your mouth.
(Proverbs 6:2)

The enemy will attempt to use negative and critical people to pull down, demoralize, and discourage individuals, families, workplaces, and churches. One of the wicked one's most effective weapons is discouragement. If left unchecked, it can spread like a cancer.

May you and I live by, and speak God's Word in all situations.

My son, give attention to my words; Incline your ear to my sayings,
Do not let them depart from your eyes;
Keep them in the midst of your heart; For they are life to those who find them, And health to all their flesh.
Keep your heart with all diligence,
For out of it spring the issues of life.
Put away from you a deceitful mouth, and put perverse lips far from you.
(Proverbs 4:20-24)

Always remember, loved one; that every good thing that we receive from God, comes as a direct result of Christ's sacrificial death for you and me on Calvary's cross.

- CHAPTER 2 -

CHANGES

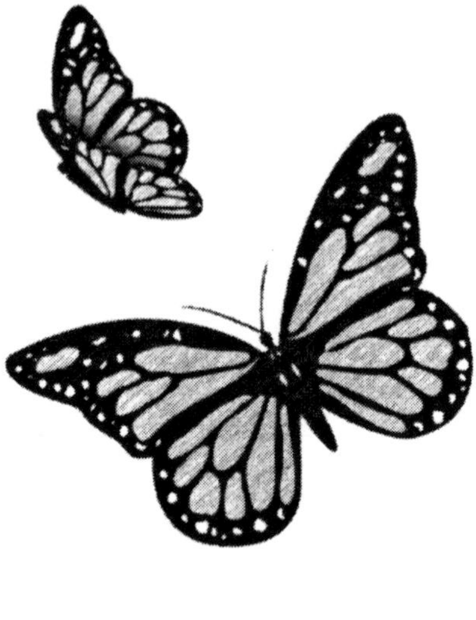

God is doing new things in our day. He's always current with the times.

*Do not remember the former things,
Nor consider the things of old.
Behold, I will do a new thing,
Now it shall spring forth;
Shall you not know it?
I will even make a road in the wilderness
And rivers in the desert.*
(Isaiah 43:18-19)

So many believers have a difficult time dealing with change. They don't like that which is new or different because they're unwilling to make the changes that may be required of them. We must understand that if you and I are going to flow with the Spirit of God, we must be willing to change whenever He commands it to be done. This passage from Isaiah 43 says that we must perceive when God is doing a new thing. Not only that, we need to recognize that it is God doing it, and that it's incumbent upon us to obey at that moment. The bottom line is that you and I must commit ourselves to the new thing God wants done. Our Father is looking for people who won't dig in their heels and resist change, but will flow with it.

But if it is of God, you cannot overthrow it—lest you even be found to fight against God.
(Acts 5:39)

Multitudes of God's children on this planet want their will to be done, rather than His. I know, I've been there and done that, much to my own detriment. Though I am one of those people who actually thrive on change, on occasion, I've rebelled against a few of those changes. Oftentimes, accepting change is hard on the ego and on one's flesh. Nevertheless, you'll need to put down the flesh and submit to the Lordship of Christ. Determine in your own heart that you're going to flow with God. Being a Christ-follower means that we must become flexible to anything and everything He desires to do in and through our lives.

The story of the children of Israel moving with the cloud of God found in Exodus 40:34-38 is a valuable example to us today. Had they not remained alert, the Israelites would have missed the leading and flow of God. Today, in New Testament times, we don't have the cloud as they did, but we are led by the Holy Spirit. The Apostle Paul admonishes us in his Epistles to *be led of the Spirit* (Galatians 5:18) and *let us also walk in the Spirit* (Galatians 5:25).

Jesus Himself told us, *However, when He, the Spirit of truth, has come, He will guide you into all truth; for He will not speak on His own authority, but whatever He hears He will speak; and He will tell you things to come.* (John 16:13)

It is vital that we always have our spirits attuned to the leading of the Holy Spirit. If you and I will listen and be quick to obey, we will always be in the right place at the right time. We'll also then be sensitive to any adjustments and course corrections He instructs us to make. The worst thing that can happen is that we become so locked in to "how we've always done it here," so that we are unwilling to change.

We read in Numbers chapter nine how important it was for the children of Israel to be sensitive and obedient to change. The Lord God commanded they drive their stakes into the ground tight enough to make the tents secure, but also loose enough to be able to pull them up and break camp at a moment's notice. Today, the Lord wants us to be willing and obedient where change is concerned, even at the risk of appearing foolish to others. We must be willing and obedient to change even when others misunderstand, or when we are be mocked and persecuted because of it. Wouldn't you rather be popular with God than with man? I definitely would. Do not resist change when it is specifically directed by God.

Jesus said, *New wine must be put into new wineskins, and both are preserved.* (Luke 5:38). The word "new" means something not seen or done in this way before. The wineskins spoken of by our Lord represents the container or the method for delivering God's message to His people. Oral Roberts made a powerful statement long ago. He said, "Never become married to methods." The Word of God is eternal and it never changes, but the method for getting the message out can change many times.

New wine must be put into new wineskins, and both are preserved.'
(Luke 5:38)

If you and I desire to be in the flow of the Holy Spirit and what God is doing, we must then change when He tells is to change. In this same passage from Luke, our Lord tells us that some will not like the change. *For he says, 'the old is better'* (v. 39). Are you willing to break away from the old when God introduces the new?

There are two important keys to be learned

from Paul in regard to change. The first is to possess a spirit of readiness or anticipation. *Be ready in every good work.* (Titus 3:1) Do not "dilly-dally" around when you know God is calling for a change. Secondly, be willing and able to adjust in any and every situation.

To the weak I became as weak, that I might win the weak. I have become all things to all men, that I might by all means save some. Now this I do for the gospel's sake, that I may be partaker of it with you. (1 Corinthians 9:22-23)

To be sure, we are not talking about compromise here. The Apostle Paul would never compromise the message nor his own convictions, but was willing to adjust to every situation so that he would always be effective in life and ministry.

If you and I will apply these scriptural principles to our lives, then we will always be in the flow of what God is doing. Riding the wave of the Holy Spirit should be our utmost desire.

- CHAPTER 3 -

WORRIED SICK

Human beings worry. We worry about a myriad of things. The truth of the matter is that worry is very unhealthy and makes you totally miserable. It accomplishes nothing whatsoever. Someone once said that worrying is stewing without doing.

The greatest sermon ever preached was the Sermon on the Mount that Jesus delivered in Matthew's Gospel, chapters 5 through 7. In chapter 6, the Master gave us some reasons why we are not to worry because it's the truth that sets us free. I think the hardest command in all the Bible to obey is not *don't commit adultery, do not murder*, or *do not steal*, but it's the one in Philippians 4:6 that says, *…do not worry about anything.* That one is hard! If God tells you not to worry about anything, he will make a way for you to accomplish just that. It's interesting to note that the definition for "worry" is from an English root word which means "to choke" or "to strangle." And let's face it, worry strangles the life out of you. It chokes off any joy from your soul. In the New Testament Greek, the meaning of worry or fear literally means "a divided mind." There's a soulish tug of war raging inside you that causes unspeakable misery. It's called *fear*.

So, what does Jesus tell us about worry and fear? First of all, worry is irrational.

That is why I tell you not to worry about everyday life—whether you have enough food and drink, or enough clothes to wear. Isn't life more than food, and your body more than clothing?
(Matthew 6:25, NLT)

Worry is irrational. Maybe you're getting ready to go out for an evening of fine dining and the theatre. A lady might open her loaded walk-in closet and exclaim, "I don't have a thing to wear!" She might put a last-minute snag in her pantyhose and just lose it. During this time her guy might be sneaking a snack before leaving the house, and spilling cold pizza down the front of his crisp white shirt. "Oh man! This stinks! That's my only nice shirt and she's going to kill me. The evening's ruined!" Worry makes no sense because we tend fret over our petty materialistic issues. We worry about the wrong thing. Jesus is saying that if you are going to worry about something, then worry about what is eternal and not temporary. We tend to get upset over the dumbest things. Hey, if you can change a situation, change it. If you can't, don't worry about it.

Worry is not only irrational, it is also illogical and unreasonable because it always exaggerates and magnifies the problem. If you've gotten into hot water with the boss at work, you start worrying about it and it becomes bigger and bigger in your mind. Each time you dwell on it the problem increases in size—until finally, you believe the entire world is against you. Worry is irrational because it throws everything completely out of proportion.

Second, worry is not natural.

Look at the birds. They don't plant or harvest or store food in barns, for your heavenly Father feeds them. And aren't you more valuable to him than they are? Can all your worries add a single moment to your life? And why worry about your clothing? Look at the lilies of the field and how they grow. They don't work or make their clothing, yet Solomon in all his glory was not dressed as beautifully as they are.
(Matthew 6:26-29, NLT)

God is saying here that animals and plants don't worry. The only thing in the entirety of all of creation that worries is man—human beings! Psalm 145:16 says that God *satisfies the desire of every living thing.* All creation trusts God, except man. Our Lord says that worry is irrational and it's just not natural. Human beings were not created to worry.

I've heard lots of people say, "I'm just a born worrier," as if that were a badge of honor. My response to them is, No you're not a born worrier. You learned how to worry. You learned from your parents, friends, significant others, and all kinds of folks around you. The good news is that since worry is learned, it can also be unlearned. You don't have to cling to it with a death-grip. Anxiety doesn't have to mess up the rest of your life.

Fear and worry takes a serious toll on the human body. We give ourselves ulcers, migraines, and all sorts of maladies resulting from mind-numbing worry. How many times have you or someone said, "I am just worried sick?" That's exactly what you do. Worry can make you very sick.

Worry weighs a person down; an encouraging word cheers a person up.
(Proverbs 12:25, NLT)

A peaceful heart leads to a healthy body...
(Proverbs 14:30, NLT)

Worry causes more fatigue than it does work because lots of folks worry more than they work. The obvious solution would be for us to pray more and worry less. If you prayed as much as you worried, there'd be a lot less to worry about. Our heavenly Father knows our needs. He tells us, "Dear child, I will take care of you."

Third, worry is useless.

In verse 27, Jesus asks, *Can all your worries add a single moment to your life?* Worry cannot make you taller or skinnier. It surely can't make you live longer. If anything, worry will cut your life short. It's like sitting in your rocking chair…a whole lot of motion, and no forward progress. So why worry? It only makes you miserable. It'll make you crazy.

- **Question #1:** When you worry about your past, does that change it? Of course it doesn't.
- **Question #2:** When you worry about the future, does that control it? No way.

Jesus said that worry is not natural and it's futile.

Let's take a look at the 30th verse in Matthew, chapter 6:

And if God cares so wonderfully for wildflowers that are here today and thrown into the fire tomorrow, He will certainly care for you. Why do you have so little faith? (NLT)

God is reassuringly telling us, "I'm your Father. I am your Source of supply. Do not worry about where your next pay check is coming from. Just trust Me."

He cares for us because we are so valuable in His eyes.

And this same God Who takes care of me will supply all your needs from His glorious riches, which have been given to us in Christ Jesus.

(Philippians 4:19, NLT)

Does that include mortgage payments? Yes. My car payments? Yes. My doctor bills? Yep. How about new shoes? Of course. So why in heaven's name are you worrying? I'll tell you what fear and worry is, and here's the bottom line: If you're full of fear and worry, you are really not trusting God. You have a misunderstanding of what God is really like. If I misunderstand what God is like then I can't trust him, and if I can't trust him then I will be filled with fear and worry.

Who do you think God is? Do you think God will do what he's promised? We always get into trouble when we doubt God's unfailing love. If God can be trusted with my eternal salvation, can't he be trusted for everything else?

So many tell God, "Father, I give You my life. Save me from an eternity in hell. Solve my biggest problem and forgive all my sins, and take me to heaven as I make Jesus Christ the Lord of my life, *but* I'll take care of all my finances." How dumb does that sound? If God saved your soul, He solved your biggest problem. Any other issues you may have are miniscule by comparison. You don't need to worry, friend. God will help you with those problems of yours.

If you will, imagine you're out hiking along a deserted dirt road. It's hotter than blazes, you're dog-tired, and your back-pack is weighing you down. A pickup truck comes along, and the man inside offers you a ride. Hallelujah! You say, "Wow. Thank you!" So you get into the truck but you keep you cumbersome back-pack on your back. The driver of the pick-up says, "Hey, why don't you take that weight off your back and throw it into the bed of the truck?" And you respond, "No, no, it's enough for you just to carry me. I'll carry the backpack."

We do that with God, don't we? We say, "God, you go ahead and take care of all the really big stuff, and *I'll* handle the family crisis myself...I'll handle the job issues...I'll carry the health problems." God exclaims, "What are you trying to do? I said in Philippians 4:19 that I'll supply all your needs— spiritual, emotional, physical, financial, and relational — if you'll trust Me."

Finally, may I say that fear and worry is sin. It is unchristian.

When you are full of fear and worry, you are behaving like an atheist. That's right. You're behaving as if God doesn't exist because you don't believe He'll do what He's promised to do for you. Worry is sin. Worry is unchristian. Unbelievers have every right to be worried and fearful. If I did not have a personal relationship with Jesus Christ, I'd be 'scared spitless,' not only in this world, but especially in the world to come.

However, believers should be different. We do not have to worry or be fearful because we have a heavenly Father Who's promised to supply all our needs, and to bless us. God says we act as if we were orphan children every time that we worry. In essence, we are saying, "I don't really think God will do what He's promised. I don't know if I trust what the Bible says." How often do we act as if God is unaware of our utility payment, or mortgage, those other bills, or that God's unaware of any area? Being consumed with worry, fear and not trusting God can turn you into a practical atheist because worry is playing God. Yes, when you worry like that you are playing God. You are assuming responsibility that

God never intended you to have, and you're trying to control that which cannot be controlled. It doesn't really matter how many self-help books you read that state you are the master of your life. You're not. God is the Master of your life. I cannot be anything that I want to be, but I can be all that God wants me to be, and that's where meaning, value, significance, and success come from.

What is your biggest worry? How can you successfully overcome that worry, anxiety, and fear?

We need to look no farther than the words that Jesus spoke during His Sermon on the Mount in order to defeat worry and fear in our lives. Again, let's take a look at Matthew's gospel, chapter 6, verses 32-33:

These things dominate the thoughts of unbelievers, but your heavenly Father already knows all your needs. Seek the Kingdom of God above all else, and live righteously, and He will give you everything you need. (NLT)

Above all else — give God first place in every area of your life.

Whenever I fall into the downward spiral of worry, it always indicates something is out of order in me, and something else other than God has taken first place in my life. Whichever area where God is not number one in your life will inevitably become a major source of worry for you. If God is not first place in a particular area—it may be your marriage or your career or finances, it doesn't matter what it is—wherever God isn't first; that area will become a major worry. You can count on it because nothing was ever meant to take the place of God. The commandment says, *You shall have no other gods before Me.* (Exodus 20:3, KJV)

If you allow anything to take God's place in life, you are maneuvering into a position where you're not qualified to stand, and you will reap the whirlwind. You must first get your priorities right because it simplifies your life and there will be much less to worry and fret about. If you'll put God first place, and make Jesus the Lord of your life, He will take care of all these other things: That's His promise to you. Stop living for things and start living for God. Anytime we love anything in this world more than God, that thing or person will become a real source of worry because you're afraid you might lose it. Put God *first* and you'll find true peace.

The next thing Jesus said to do in order to conquer worry and fear is to live one day at a time.

So don't worry about tomorrow, for tomorrow will bring its own worry. Today's trouble is enough for today. (Matthew 6:34, NLT)

That verse makes sense, doesn't it? Don't freak out about tomorrow. Don't open your umbrella until it starts raining. Don't worry: Focus on today. Never worry about yesterday or tomorrow, because today is the tomorrow you worried about yesterday.

Like an old song once said, "One day at a time, Sweet Jesus." You see, by always worrying about tomorrow's problems, you miss out on today's blessings. In Matthew 6:11, Jesus teaches us to pray, *Give us today our daily bread* because he wants you to depend on him one day at a time. It's totally fine to plan for tomorrow, but you've got to only focus on today. Trust in the Lord moment by moment.

The third thing Jesus instructs us to do to

conquer a spirit of fear and worry is to trust God to care for the things beyond your control.

Put God first, live one day at a time, and trust the Lord to care for things that are beyond my control. Worry and trust cannot live in the same heart. And worry will camp out in your heart until you invite faith back in the front door; and at that moment, worry and fear will high-tail it out the back door! You will have to make a quality decision and ask yourself, "Am I going to trust my worries or am I going to trust God?" There are many things way beyond your control but you can trust God, because they're not beyond his control and he'll help you.

Don't worry about anything; instead, pray about everything. Tell God what you need, and thank Him for all He has done. Then you will experience God's peace, which exceeds anything we can understand. His peace will guard your hearts and minds as you live in Christ Jesus.
(Philippians 4:6-7, NLT)

Don't panic, pray. These are the only two choices. We will either panic or we will pray when we face the difficulties in life. Friend, if it isn't worth praying about, it isn't worth worrying about. If you and I prayed as much as we worried, we have a lot less to worry about. Wouldn't we? May I suggest that you read you divine insurance policy? Get into your Bible and find out what belongs to you in Christ. There are literally thousands of great and precious promises that are yours for the asking. When you purchase an insurance policy, you carefully read what the policy covers. Once you understand what's covered, you don't worry about it anymore, because if something happens, the insurance policy will take care of it...but you need to know what's in the policy! God has made so many promises to you in the Bible, but you can't claim them if you don't know them. Study God's Word. Devour it. Feed your spirit by it, so when the hard times do come, God will have them there for you.

Since God didn't spare even His own Son for us but gave Him up for us, won't He surely give us everything else?"
(Romans 8:32, NLT)

If God loved me enough to send Jesus, His only begotten Son, to die on the cross for me, don't you think He loves me enough to care for every other need in my life?

Why not talk to God about your worries and fears right now?

- CHAPTER 4 -

EYEBALL TO EYEBALL WITH FEAR

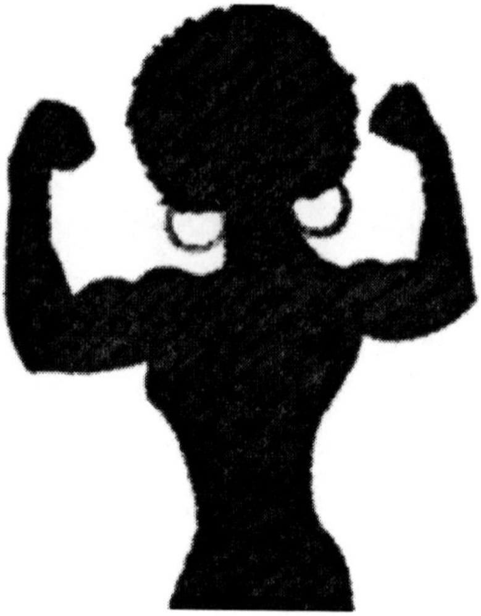

For the Lord spoke thus to me with a strong hand, and instructed me that I should not walk in the way of this people, saying:

Do not say, "A conspiracy,"
Concerning all that this people call a conspiracy,
Nor be afraid of their threats, nor be troubled.
The Lord of hosts, Him you shall hallow;
Let Him be your fear, and let Him be your dread.
(Isaiah 8:11-13)

Throughout the entirety of the Bible, God repeatedly commands and reassures His people to "Be not afraid, for I am with you." The Lord does not want us to be in bondage to fear because fear brings torment. The Lord loves us and desires to bless us above and beyond all we can ask or think or imagine.

I want you to see from God's Word that those who are followers of Jesus Christ do not need to be fearful of the things that unbelievers fear.

…God has not given us a spirit of fear and timidity, but of power, love, and self-discipline.
(2 Timothy 1:7, NLT)

God repeatedly tells us we can live victoriously, strong in the Lord and in the power of his might. He has promised to never leave or forsake us, regardless of what happens.

We've all at one time or another experienced starting to step out in faith, when just the thought of the size of the mountain before us makes fear rise up inside. That source of fear is none other than the enemy of your soul, Satan, himself.

However, 1 John 4:18 reassures us that:

Such (God's) *love has no fear; because perfect love expels all fear. If we are afraid, it is for fear of punishment, and this shows we have not fully experienced His perfect love.* (NLT)

The adversary brings fear and torment into the hearts of people to make them doubtful and miserable. He believes he can prevent us from fulfilling God will and destiny for our lives.

You can strike a death-blow to fear by building up your faith on the Word of God.

Do not be afraid or discouraged, for the Lord will personally go ahead of you. He will be with you. He will neither fail you nor abandon you. (Deuteronomy 31:8, NLT)

We need to keep close watch over what we believe with our hearts and speak out of our mouths. Romans 10:17 tells us that,

Faith comes by hearing, and hearing by the Word of God.

We must learn and profess aloud and in power Scriptures like these, and drink them in like water when we are thirsty. When we open our mouths and boldly proclaim what the Lord says to us and about us, God's Word will empower us to overcome the fears that bring torment.

And we are confident that He hears us whenever we ask for anything that pleases Him. And since we know that He hears us when we make our requests,

we also know that He will give us what we ask for.
(1 John 5:15, NLT)

I am fully persuaded that one of the most important things we can do during our prayer time is to confess God's Word. If at any time we are trying to avoid confronting our fears, we need to pray and ask God to do for us what he has promised in the Word, and go before us to pave the way for what we need. James teaches that we have not because we ask not (James 4:2), and Jesus tells us to ask, seek, and knock (Matthew 7:7). You can believe that whatever happens, it will turn out for your good in accordance with God's perfect will for your life.

How would you react if God instructed you to pack up everything you own and leave your community, your family, and your comfortable home, and then head out to who knows where? A little scared?

This is exactly what God told Abram to do, and I'm sure it frightened him somewhat. That's when God began telling him, "Don't be afraid."

The Lord said to Abram, "Leave your native country, your relatives, and your father's family, and go to the land that I will show you."
(Genesis 12:1, NLT).

Anyone who dares to step out in faith and do something great for God, will need to hear the Lord say regularly, "Don't be afraid." Friend, even if your knees are knocking, your mouth is as dry as a desert, and feel as if you'll crumble into a million pieces, just stand tall and say. "Father, strengthen me! I'm standing on your promise to me. This is what you've told me to do. I'm determined that my life will not be ruled by fear or doubt. I am only moved by God's Word!"

One cannot wish fear away. Fear must be dealt with and confronted with the Word of God. You address and confront and overcome fear by meditating, obeying, and boldly speaking God's Word ourselves, and resist fear in the power of the Holy Spirit.

Sometime later the Lord spoke to Abram in a vision and said to him, 'Do not be afraid, Abram, for I will protect you, and your reward will be great.
(Genesis 15:1, NLT)

Back in Genesis 12:1, the Lord instructed Abram to "Pack up and leave everyone you know and everything you're comfy with, and go to a place I will show you." Had Abram given in to fear, the rest of the story would have never taken place. He would never have experienced God's protection, increased prosperity, and ultimate reward.

There is dynamic power in the Word of God. Isn't it time to believe it, speak it, obey it, and receive it?

Fear is from the adversary — Satan. Fear does not come from God. The only attitude a Spirit-filled believer can adopt toward fear is that, "Fear is not from my God, and I refuse to allow it into my heart and life. I will not put up with it. I will confront and defeat fear in the name of Jesus!"

Satan skillfully uses fear in order to inhibit followers of Christ from coming under His Lordship. We know that our loving Heavenly Father is ever so gentle with His children as He works through us to bring us out of bondage into freedom. The Bible is full of "Be not afraid(s)!" Dear one, keep moving forward. Do not retreat. Do not run from fear. God is your Deliverer. Confront the spirit of fear eyeball to eyeball through power, prayer, and mountain moving faith!

*"Let the words of my mouth,
and the meditation of my heart,
be acceptable in Thy sight,
O Lord, my strength and my
Redeemer."*
(Psalm 19:14, KJV)

- CHAPTER 5 -

SPEAK!

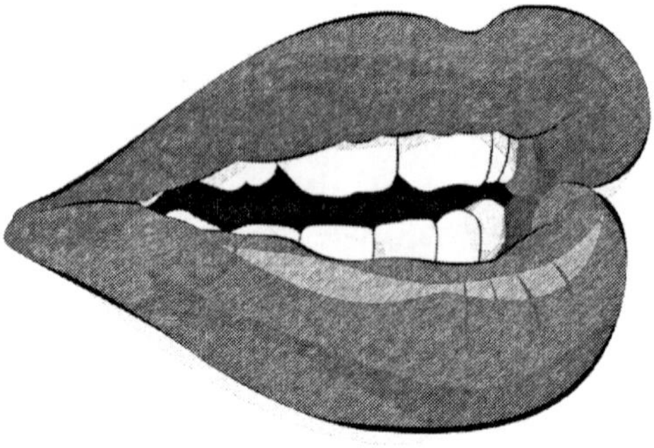

Jesus answered and said to them, "Have faith in God. For assuredly, I say to you, whoever says to this mountain, 'Be removed and be cast into the sea,' and does not doubt in his heart, but believes that those things he says will be done, he will have whatever he says. Therefore, I say to you, whatever things you ask when you pray, believe that you receive them, and you will have them."
(Mark 11:22-24)

Three times in this passage, Jesus reiterated that those things which we say are important...and powerful. Why are our words so important? It's because the Word of God tells us that death and life are in the power of your tongue. Yes, death and life.

Death and life are in the power of the tongue, And those who love it will eat its fruit.
(Proverbs 18:21)

Powerful. In fact, if you'll backtrack to Mark 11:22 and look closely, it says, *whoever says to this mountain, 'Be removed and be cast into the sea,' and does not doubt in his heart, but believes that those things he says will be done, he will have whatever he says.* Jesus mentions only one time to "believe" but three times to "say." If the Lord spoke of the importance of "saying" three times, then we can take it to the bank!

Why are the words that we speak so vitally important? It is because what you say is exactly what you are going to believe — for better or worse, blessing or cursing, life or death. What you say will either bring you faith, or it will cause doubt and unbelief to rise up in your heart and life. It will come to pass. Jesus told us that we will have whatever we say. Whatever you dwell on and consistently speak will come to pass. Your words have power.

Words can start major wars — between people — and entire nations. We've seen how words have divided our nation here in the USA. Words spoken with love in the right direction can bring forth reconciliation, healing, peace, and absolutely change a whole country. Words have the power to destroy multitudes of people, or they can cause lives to be changed for the better.

I've personally witnessed many men, women, and children make a change of eternal significance by believing the Word of God and accepting Jesus as their Savior and Lord. I have also seen others baptized in the Holy Spirit and even healed in their bodies. I know that as they have spoken and confessed their belief, it has changed their lives. I may never see most of these dear brothers and sisters in Christ again on this earth, but I know we shall be reunited in heaven. If they continue to speak their power, they shall see the influence of that power this side of heaven, as well.

Now that we understand something about the significance of the spoken word, we know that we can move the mountain by speaking God's Word and the thing we desire. Yes, our words are powerful, and you shall have whatever you say. So, say it. Speak it out. Call it done in the Name of Jesus and do not doubt. When is it going to happen? It'll happen when you believe!

Therefore, I say to you, whatever things you ask when you pray, believe that you receive them, and you will have them.
(Mark 11:24)

Dear one, I'm telling you, it's going to happen. Seedtime and harvest are upon you. As one preacher said, "You have a miracle in your mouth!"

The word is near you, in your mouth and in your heart (that is, the word of faith which we preach): that if you confess with your mouth the Lord Jesus and believe in your heart that God has raised Him from the dead, you will be saved.
(Romans 10:8-9)

You have to believe it in your heart. If you believe it in your heart, you are going to say it. Now remember, the enemy of our souls wants us to say other things. He wants to control your feelings and fleshly desires. However, we must renew our mind to the things of God and allow His Word to guide us daily.

May I be so bold as to say that cancer was not meant for you. Blind eyes meant for you. Deaf ears were not intended for you. Oppression was not invented by our good, good Father to come upon you in order to "teach you a lesson." Through the finished work of Jesus Christ at the cross, you and I were redeemed from the curse of the law. Jesus redeemed us from the curse of spiritual death, sickness, and poverty. They don't belong to us. We are redeemed!

So how am I going to take hold of what Jesus has provided for me, Tony? You will receive these great and precious promises by believing in your heart and boldly speaking words of faith with your mouth.

Yes, "Let the redeemed of the Lord say so!"

- CHAPTER 6 -

HUNGRY FOR MORE

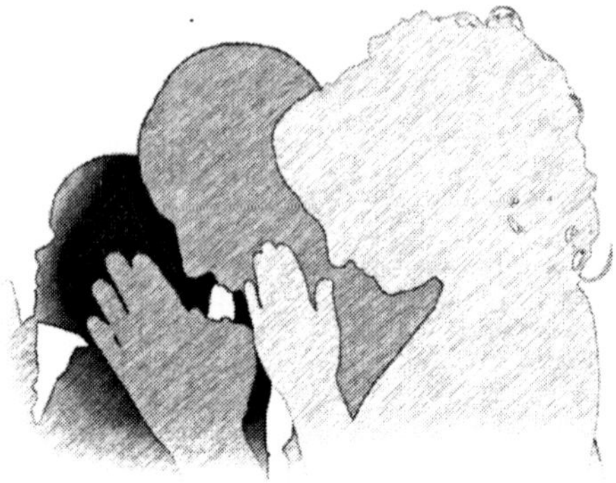

There was a point in time when the prophet Isaiah grieved over the spiritual condition of his own people. The nation as a whole was inconsistent in their walk with the Almighty. Over time, they had become lukewarm and as a result, were in desperate need of revival. It's not at all an understatement to say Isaiah was grieved to the heart.

Then he remembered the days of old,
Moses and his people, saying:
"Where is He who brought them up out of the sea
With the shepherd of His flock?
Where is He who put His Holy Spirit within them,
Who led them by the right hand of Moses,
With His glorious arm,
Dividing the water before them
To make for Himself an everlasting name,
(Isaiah 63:11-12)

The prophet wept over what he saw and began crying out for a move of God. In this passage of scripture, Isaiah recalled how God revealed Himself in Moses' day. He plead with the Lord to show mercy and revive His people again. The people were terribly rebellious and Isaiah knew they didn't deserve mercy, but he also knew that God was kind and merciful. In fact, God was so loving that if the people would make the slightest move toward Him, then He would forgive them.

I want you to know that God wants to show Himself strong. He truly desires to demonstrate His power on our behalf. He wants to show us signs and wonders. All that our Father is waiting for is someone to hunger for it. This hunger and desperation is what we see in Isaiah. The prophet hungered for a sovereign, powerful move of God.

He had an all-consuming desire for God to manifest His presence, because he knew that only a move of God could change the sinful condition that the world was mired in. Kind of sounds like our day. Doesn't it?

He cried out to the Lord, "Look down from heaven..." (v. 15)

Then he asked, "Where is the love for us that You used to show?" (TLB)

Wow! Don't you wish that more believers were this hungry for a move of God today? There would be no telling what God would do if they were.

You did awesome things beyond our highest expectations. (TLB, v. 3)

As T.D. Jakes often says, "Get ready! Get ready! Get ready!" Aren't you ready for a powerful move of God like this today? I believe our God is ready, and He is looking for somebody who is hungry for it.

For since the beginning of the world
Men have not heard nor perceived by the ear,
Nor has the eye seen any God besides You,
Who acts for the one who waits for Him.
(Isaiah 64:4)

Wouldn't you love to see God move in your city? Your state? Your nation? It's apparent He will do just that if we will just hunger for it, and ask. My friend, God will manifest His presence in our lives in direct proportion to our hunger for it.

*Blessed are those who hunger and thirst for righteousness,
For they shall be filled.*
(Matthew 5:6)

Draw near to God and He will draw near to you. Cleanse your hands, you sinners; and purify your hearts, you double-minded.
(James 4:8)

The Lord tells us plainly that He will manifest His presence and power in our lives if we will show Him that we truly desire it.

Can you really say that you're desperate like never before? You see, desperate people are willing to do whatever takes. They will pray like Jacob prayed, *I will not let go of you, unless you bless me!* (Genesis 32:26) Is this your heart's desire today? Lots of folks say they want to see a move of God, but are they willing to pay the price for it?

I love hearing and reading about the late, great Evan Roberts. Here's what he was willing to do. He declared, "I will not leave this place until God visits my nation."[1] He meant business with God and was a man with a mission. He was sick and tired of the religious status quo. Brother Roberts sought God's presence and power for his generation and cried out to Him. He later wrote, "I was taken up into divine fellowship and it changed my whole being. I reached out and touched the flame of God and now I am burning with His presence. From that moment, I knew that God was going to work in our land."[2]

The Lord graciously allowed Evan Roberts to experience His presence in direct proportion to His desperation for more of God. Isn't it about time for all of God's people to stir themselves up and seek

His face once again?

Wake up the mighty men.
(Joel 3:9)

It is high time to awake out of sleep.
(Romans 13:11)

The cry of our hearts should be as the Psalmist wrote long ago,

O God, You are my God;
Early will I seek You;
My soul thirsts for You;
My flesh longs for You
In a dry and thirsty land
Where there is no water.
So I have looked for You in the sanctuary,
To see Your power and Your glory.
(Psalm 63:1-2)

I believe with all my heart that the days of even greater works and revival are just around the corner. The Lord is just waiting on us.

Ask the Lord for rain
In the time of the latter rain.
The Lord will make flashing clouds;
He will give them showers of rain,
Grass in the field for everyone.
(Zechariah 10:1)

Let us know,
Let us pursue the knowledge of the Lord.
His going forth is established as the morning;
He will come to us like the rain,

Like the latter and former rain to the earth.
(Hosea 6:3)

It sounds like these holy men of old are describing our generation and prophesying that we can have an outpouring of the presence of God like we've never witnessed before. The only thing holding it back would be a lack of hunger on our part.

It's time to 'Arise, shine...'
(Isaiah 60:1)

The time has come for you and me...all of us...to press in. We must get out of ourselves and get into God.

For I will pour water upon him who is thirsty...
(Isaiah 44:3)

Our God goes on and says that He literally will open up the floodgates and reveal His presence like never before. Do you desire to see and experience this in your lifetime? How hungry and desperate are you for more of Him?

Settle in your own heart right now that your number one pursuit will be ...

Seek the LORD and His strength;
Seek His face evermore!
(1 Chronicles 16:11)

- CHAPTER 7 -

SAYING "YES" TO GOD'S PLAN

YES!

Till we all come to the unity of the faith and of the knowledge of the Son of God, to a perfect man, to the measure of the stature of the fullness of Christ.
(Ephesians 4:13)

Our Heavenly Father desires us to enter into the fullness of His perfect plan for our lives. He always knows what's best for His children. His plan is always with our ultimate good in mind. The time has come for us to finally be rid of all of our self-induced limitations. We also must take the limits off God because He wants to do more in our lives than we could ever imagine. Remember, no more limits! Let's be open and obedient to the leading of the Holy Spirit who leads us toward our magnificent destiny as we begin to tap into our full potential in Christ. *I will not be brought under the power of any.* (1 Corinthians 6:12)

This same verse in the New American Standard Bible says it this way: *I will not be mastered by anything.*

That sounds pretty bold, doesn't it? This is not some arrogant pronouncement. No, it is coming from a man of God who knows who he is in Christ Jesus. This was the great Apostle Paul who had made up his mind that nothing would stop him from tapping into the fullness of his potential and destiny. As far as he was concerned, there were no limitations. Paul firmly believed that the plans and purposes of God for his life would be realized, and no demon in hell would be able to stop it.

Being confident of this very thing, that He who has begun a good work in you will complete it until the day of Jesus Christ.
(Philippians 1:6)

Paul was not only supremely confident that whatever God had planned for him would happen, but here he encourages every believer to have this same confidence in God.

The Lord also assures us in Isaiah 46:10, *My purpose will be established, and I will accomplish all my good pleasure.* Do not allow the evil one to lie and try to convince you that you'll never experience God's best in your life. Shut down those lies of the devil immediately in the Name of Jesus, and stand on and declare out loud the promises of God over your life. If you will trust God and refuse to be moved by how things look in the natural, the Lord will work in and through you to full His perfect plan for your life.

It is God who works in you both to will and to do for His good pleasure.
(Philippians 2:13)

Dear one, if the Lord is working in you (and He is), show confidence in His ability to accomplished what He's promised to do in your life. It doesn't matter what failures happened in the past, just believe that God is at work within you. It's only when we begin to completely rely upon Him (despite the sins and mistakes of our past), that we tap into our full potential in Christ. He wants you and me to triumph over every form of adversity and every limitation that Satan tries to throw in our paths. We absolutely must ignore all of the "odds" against us living victorious lives.

I don't remember who this quote originated with but someone once said, "The person who eventually succeeds is not the one who holds back because of past failures, but the one who moves on in spite of his past failures." Please hear me. If you're ever going to walk in the fullness of God's perfect will and plan, then you must reach the point where you're convinced that mistakes, setbacks and failures are not permanent. Even if the adversary occasionally gets the upper hand over you, just remember that it is temporary. God will turn it around!

Do you not know this of old...
That the triumphing of the wicked is short.
(Job 20:4-5)

Loved one, don't give up and throw in the towel just because you've suffered a setback. Have you been knocked down? Then get back up. Don't believe the devil's lies that success is not in your future. Pick up and read your Bible and you'll find that God worked with and helped people who failed, especially when it seemed that they would never experience His best upon their lives.

Moses was a murderer, and God made him a deliverer. Rahab was a harlot, but God used her to help bring His people into their promised land. Jonah ran like a coward from adversity and hardship, but God turned him into a powerful missionary. Saul of Taurus was a vicious persecutor of Christians, but God turned him into a great apostle.

It doesn't matter how many times you may have blown it in the past. God declares that His grace is sufficient! Far too many Christians today do not live out the fullness of God's plan simply because they've been conditioned to believe the wrong things about themselves. These are lies from the enemy that have bound them.

I heard a story from a preacher years ago that immediately hit home with me at the time. He gave a true illustration about circus elephants from years gone by. If you've ever been to a circus during your lifetime, then you may remember seeing large elephants tied to a wooden stake with only a thin rope. However, the baby elephant is tied to a metal stake with a chain. The reason for this training is that baby elephants are constantly trying to run away. If the stake is driven far into the ground and the chain is strong, the baby elephant eventually will stop pulling and grow resigned to the fact that he can't run away. Once that happens, then the metal stake and chain are replaced with a wooden stake and a rope. Very sad, isn't it?

What has happened? The baby elephant has now been conditioned to believe that he cannot get away, and accepts his limitations.

Even sadder…This is exactly what has happened to so many followers of Jesus Christ. They've been conditioned to believe that they will never be better off than they are right now.

Think about it. If that elephant ever decides, "Hey, I'm not staying bound up like this any longer," then that little rope and skimpy wooden stake will not hold him back. The very same is true with the people of God. If we finally decide to become everything God says we can be, then the wicked one will can no longer keep us bound with lies and defeat.

Jesus told us in Matthew's Gospel, 17:20: *…and nothing shall be impossible to you.*

My friend, you will only enjoy the fullness of God's good plan for your life when you make the quality decision to agree with what God says about you. Please stop trying to justify why you have limitations, and start overcoming them with your faith in what God and His Word say about you.

The dream and desire to possess God's best for your life is great, but dreaming and desiring alone are not enough. You must stir yourself up right now, today, and inform the evil one, once and for all, that he will not run roughshod over you any longer. Get desperate and single-minded on what God says belongs to you.

Remember Blind Bartimaeus? This dear man made up his mind that nothing or no one was going to hold him back from Jesus. When the Lord came to his village, Bartimaeus determined that he was going to receive his healing no matter what anyone else thought about it. When the people tried to discourage him and shut him up, the Bible says, *He cried out all the more* (Mark 10:48). The Message Bible says, *Many tried to hush him up, but he yelled all the louder.*

His faith and desperation got Bartimaeus everything he needed from the Lord Jesus Christ. Yes, it did! It will get you everything that God says is yours as well.

- REFERENCES -

CHAPTER 1

[1]Swaggart, Jimmy. *Message Of The Cross, The.* Baton Rouge, Louisiana: Jimmy Swaggart Ministries, 2013

[2]Ibid.

[3]Ibid.

CHAPTER 6

[1]Phillips, Thomas. *Welsh Revival, The: Its Origin and Development.* London, England: Banner of Truth Trust, 1996.

[2]Ibid.

- ABOUT THE AUTHOR -

Rev. Anthony Sluzas is a traveling evangelist and revivalist. He is the founder of Your Place Of Grace Ministries, headquartered in Morgantown, West Virginia. His testimony is one of deliverance from emotional and physical abuse which he experienced as a child in parochial school, and substance abuse as a young aspiring actor/musician in Hollywood. While there, Anthony played several tiny bits on the sitcoms, *Three's Company, The Two of Us*, and appeared in numerous live theatrical productions.

He crashed and burned emotionally and spiritually in 1987, but the following year experienced a radical transformation in his heart and life when he accepted Jesus as his Lord and Savior while listening to E.V. Hill on TBN. God has worked miracles in Anthony's life and He can do the same for anyone and everyone through Jesus Christ.

Anthony served as lead Pastor in several Assemblies of God churches from 1994-2010. Since 2010, Anthony has ministered from America's east coast to west coast and points in between. Anthony preaches and teaches the Message of Grace and Faith through the Cross of Christ. He is called to win souls for Christ, and he focuses on God's Word in the areas of forgiveness, healing and deliverance. Anthony loves to serve Pastors, no matter the denomination, through prayer and a hand of friendship because he too was a Pastor for years. Now, for the past seven years, Anthony Sluzas has worked as a traveling Evangelist and Revivalist. His heart's desire is to minister to and point the way for those whom the world considers "lost causes" just like he was, to the Lord Jesus Christ.

For more information about Your Place of Grace Ministries, visit Anthony Sluzas' website at YOURPLACEOFGRACE.COM. Also, be sure to download the "Your Place of Grace" app, available in both the apple and Google play stores online.